Celebrate 5 days of Diwali

© Copyright

All rights reserved. No parts of this book may be reproduced, stored, recorded, photocopied or in any form or means without the permission of the Author and Publisher.

References:
Google, Wikipedia, Natgeokids.com

Earth Ras Publications

Paperback | Hardcover | eBook
Globally on Amazon

Disclaimer

This book aims to educate and inform readers about the significance of Diwali. While efforts have been made to provide accurate information, it should be noted that there may be variations or different interpretations of the mythological stories associated with the festival in India and other parts of the world. It is important to respect and not offend anyone's sentiments towards the culture and festival.

How many days is Diwali celebrated?

Contents

- What is Diwali?
- How is it celebrated?
- What is its significance?
- How many days is Diwali celebrated?
- Day 1 - Dhanteras
- Day 2 - Choti Diwali
- Day 3 - Diwali
- Day 4 - Govardhan Puja and Annakut
- Day 5 - Bhai Dooj
- Healthy Laddoo Recipe

Review:
Your feedback is important for us to deliver the best content to enrich children's cultural knowledge of today's diverse world. We would greatly appreciate if you could leave feedback on Amazon. You can reach the book page by scanning the QR code below. Many thanks in advance!

Earth Ras Publications

This book is a

special Diwali gift to:

_____

Note by the Publisher:
We aim to provide a wide range of books on culture, festivals, and mindfulness for children and grownups as well. Readers can expect to enjoy a delightful blend of entertainment, education, and fun through our books and journals. Browse more books on the last page and SCAN the QR code to see the whole collection on Amazon.

Earth Ras Publications
Paperback | Hardcover | eBook
Globally on Amazon

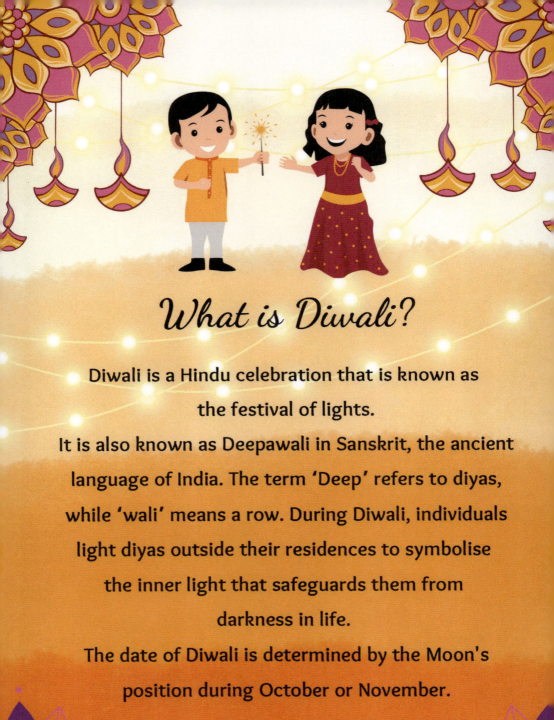

What is Diwali?

Diwali is a Hindu celebration that is known as the festival of lights.

It is also known as Deepawali in Sanskrit, the ancient language of India. The term 'Deep' refers to diyas, while 'wali' means a row. During Diwali, individuals light diyas outside their residences to symbolise the inner light that safeguards them from darkness in life.

The date of Diwali is determined by the Moon's position during October or November.

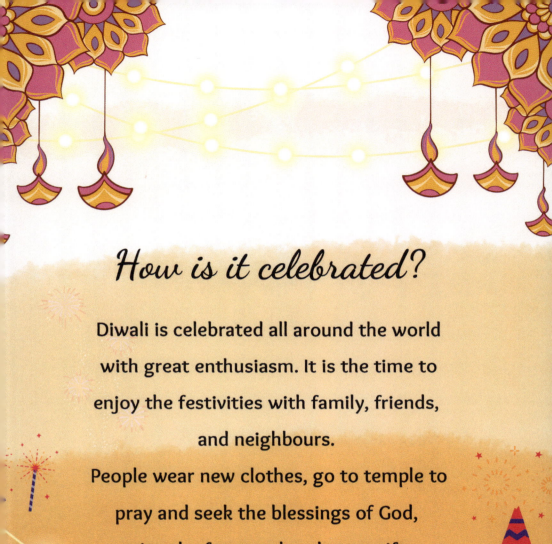

How is it celebrated?

Diwali is celebrated all around the world with great enthusiasm. It is the time to enjoy the festivities with family, friends, and neighbours.
People wear new clothes, go to temple to pray and seek the blessings of God, enjoy the feast and exchange gifts with each other.
Nonetheless, the fireworks and firecrackers are great fun too.

What is its significance?

On this day, Lord Ram returned to his kingdom known as Ayodhya, with his wife Sita and brother Laxman, after killing the ten-headed evil King - Ravan.
People lit thousands of clay and oil lamps to welcome him.
That is why it is called the festival of lights and also celebrated as the victory of good over bad.

How many days is Diwali celebrated?

Diwali is a 5-day festival

Day 1 is called Dhanteras. (Dhan-te-ras)

Day 2 is called Choti Diwali. (Cho-tee)

Day 3 is the main Diwali day. (Dee-wali)

Day 4 is known for Govardhan puja and Annakut. (Go-var-dhan)(An-na-kut)

Day 5 is called Bhai-Dooj. (Bha-yee, Doo-j)

Day 1

Dhanteras

This is the first day of Diwali. People do deep cleaning of their houses. Dhanteras is considered a good day to buy gold, metal, jewellery, utensils and clothes. People perform puja in their offices, homes and businesses to seek Goddess Laxmi's blessings.

(Dhan-te-ras)

Day 2

Choti Diwali

Families adorn their homes with lanterns, diyas, and beautiful rangoli. In the evening, they perform a small puja with clay diyas, which are then placed in all the corners of the house.

(Cho-tee)   (ran-go-lee)

Day 3

Diwali and Laxmi puja

This is the main festival day.
Worshipping Goddess Laxmi who is the deity
of wealth and abundance, is a ritual performed by all.
Offering her homemade food, sweets and
many delicacies to please her and invoke her blessings.
In the evening, everyone puts on their new outfits,
lights the oil or clay lamps and
prays to the Goddess Laxmi.
Welcoming guests with sweets and
gifts is a normal tradition.

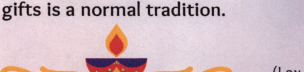

(Dee-wali)   (Lax-mee)

Day 3

Diwali and Laxmi puja

On Diwali day, people celebrate the festival by inviting and meeting extended family members, friends and neighbours. They offer food and sweets to them. Light diyas and do fireworks together. Diwali is the biggest Hindu festival and people love to give gifts to their loved ones.

Day 4

Govardhan puja

In Lord Krishna's village, Gokul - once it rained heavily which caused much chaos in the daily lives of the villagers. Seeing this, Lord Krishna through his divine power, lifted up the mountain called Govardhan on his little finger to save everyone from the downpour till it stopped raining.
Govardhan puja symbolises that Lord Krishna will always be there to protect you from all your miseries and obstacles in life.

(Go-var-dhan)

Day 4

Annakut

Devotees offer Lord Krishna with conically shaped multi-grain foods as a symbol of Govardhan Hill, renewing their faith and respect for God.

(An-na-kut)
'Ann' means grains and 'Kut' is the process of milling and preparing the grains

Day 5

Bhai - Dooj

On the final day of Diwali, there is a celebration of the strong bond between brothers and sisters. Sisters pray for their brothers' long, happy, and healthy lives by applying a 'tilak' on their forehead and feeding them with sweets and delicious food.

In return, brothers pledge to always support and love their sisters, and give them gifts as a token of their affection.

(Bha-ee) (Doo-j)

Recipe

Healthy Dry fruit/nut Laddoo for children

Please be aware that this product is not suitable for individuals with nut allergies.

Method:

This is the easiest recipe for which even children can make with an adult's supervision.

First, roast the dry fruits/nuts in a pan.

Now chop them or just whizz them up in a grinder.

Take (pitted) dates, dry figs and apricots and put them in a grinder with the dried nuts.

Add 1 tsp of chocolate powder to it.

Mix well. Now roll the mixture into small balls.

They are ready to eat!

Earth Ras Publications

Paperback | Hardcover | eBook
Globally on Amazon

Festive books from the Publisher

Engaging and Enriching

Cultural Awareness

Learning with Fun

Featured in The South Asian Times, New York

Featured in The South Asian Times, New York

Amazon UK

Amazon US

Paperbacks and E-books available worldwide on all Amazon marketplaces

Printed in Great Britain
by Amazon